Jackie O.

A LIFE IN PICTURES

Jackie O.
A LIFE IN PICTURES

ELIZABETH KANE

BARNES
& NOBLE
BOOKS

NEW YORK

A BARNES & NOBLE BOOK

ISBN 0-7607-5940-5

Produced by Atlantic Publishing

Printed and bound in China by SNP Leefung Printers Limited

1 3 5 7 9 10 8 6 4 2

Photo Credits:
All pictures courtesy of Corbis except as listed below:
Associated Newspapers:
2, 8, 43, 44, 45, 46 top and bottom, 47 top, 48 bottom, 52 top, 62, 67, 68 top and bottom, 69, 71 bottom,
77, 78, 80, 82, 83 top, 84, 85, 86, 92 top, 94, 95

Dedication

For J.K., who was with us all too fleetingly.

CONTENTS

Introduction

Opposite: Jackie was regarded as one of the world's most beautiful women, yet as a child she was riddled with insecurity and suffered from poor self-image. Her defense mechanism was to develop an emotional detachment, and the wearing of dark glasses was just one of the strategies she employed for keeping the world at arm's length.

Above: The golden couple became a golden family with the birth of Caroline in 1957. The Kennedys were feted like movie stars, and on the campaign trail Jackie invariably stole the show.

The adjective "regal" was used to describe Jacqueline Bouvier long before she met John F. Kennedy. Beautiful, intelligent, and cultured, Jackie emerged in the late 1940s as a young debutante with the world at her feet. The one thing she didn't want, as she noted in her graduation yearbook, was to be simply "a housewife," and her contemporaries marked her out for much greater things.

Jackie's upbringing was far from idyllic, however. She was filled with self-doubt and insecurity, the product of being witness to her parents' tempestuous marriage. She was constantly criticized by her stern mother, Janet, with whom she never enjoyed an easy relationship. Meanwhile, she adored her rakish father, "Black Jack" Bouvier, ever forgiving of his fecklessness and philandering. To Jackie, his irresistible, life-affirming qualities far outweighed his failings. Unsurprisingly, Byron was a favorite poet and she would be drawn to men like her father, who were somewhat "dangerous to know."

Jacqueline Bouvier met John F. Kennedy at a dinner party in June 1951. The playboy image of one of the most eligible bachelors in the country was a magnet for Jackie, not a deterrent. Jack Kennedy represented the ultimate antidote to the low self-esteem that her mother had done so much to foster. Jack thought her beautiful, erudite, and classy—the ideal wife for a politician already being tipped as a rising star.

They were married on September 12, 1953. It was a union in which love, commitment, and tenderness would be tempered with acts of callousness and infidelity. In childhood Jackie had developed the ability to block out words and deeds that caused her emotional distress, and this served her well in adulthood.

Jackie inherited the title of First Lady from Mamie Eisenhower after J.F.K.'s election victory on November 8, 1960. During the thousand days of his presidency she brought glamor and elegance to the White House. The Kennedys enjoyed movie star status, and Jackie was always the center of attention. On a visit to France in 1961 the president recognized as much when he self-deprecatingly described himself as "the man who accompanied Jackie Kennedy to Paris." The first lady captivated a succession of world leaders, and in a solo trip to meet the heads of the governments of India and Pakistan in 1962, she showed she had sure-footed diplomatic skills to match her beauty and grace.

The way in which Jackie bore the events of November 22, 1963, in Dallas, cemented her place in the affection of the American people and won universal admiration. Even in the wake of tragedy Jackie remained every inch a queen. A thirty-four-year-old widow with two children to raise, Jackie set about rebuilding her life. By 1968 she was enthused by the prospect of Bobby Kennedy carrying on Jack's work in the White House. His assassination in June of that year had a profound effect on Jackie. Security again became the overriding concern, and she resolved to remove her children from theviolent atmosphere that seemed to pervade the United States.

Jackie married Greek shipping tycoon Aristotle Onassis on October 20, 1968. Once again she had chosen a rich, powerful, older man with a magnetic personality. Following Onassis's death in 1975, Jackie returned to America. She took up paid employment and found new love, this time choosing dependability and shared interests over dangerous attraction. Most important, she nurtured her children, Caroline and John, Jr., through to adulthood. The latter years of her life were thus taken up with the preoccupations of most middle-aged women. But the mystique surrounding Jackie meant that even the everyday trappings of life were imbued with an enduring fascination. With Jackie, the public ensured that everything was elevated to the extraordinary.

Jackie Kennedy Onassis succumbed to cancer on May 19, 1994, and was buried alongside Jack in Arlington Cemetery. Although her contribution to politics was slight, Jackie was central to the Camelot idyll. The image of the Kennedy presidency was that of a golden age of poetry and power. J.F.K.'s hands may have been on the levers of power, but it was Jackie who provided the poetry.

Above: Jack and Jackie pictured two days before their wedding in September 1953. Jackie was determined that the Kennedy presidency would rise above the functional and utilitarian. It was she who gave the thousand-day administration its grace and style.

Chapter One

World at Her Feet

Above: Five-year-old Jackie competing in the annual horse show at the Southampton Riding and Hunt Club, New York. Horses would be a passion throughout her life, and were often an outlet for the emotions of a difficult childhood that had made her wary of investing in people.

Opposite: This 1953 portrait captures the serene beauty that men would find so bewitching. One of that number was stockbroker John Husted, to whom Jackie was briefly engaged in 1952. Jackie's childhood experience had left her with a craving for security—which Husted offered—but he lacked the charisma of her chief male role model, her beloved father, "Black Jack" Bouvier. Shortly after breaking off the engagement to Husted, Jackie renewed her acquaintance with Jack Kennedy, whose magnetic personality matched her father's.

Left: Jackie pictured shortly before her fourth birthday with her mother, Janet. From an early age Jackie sought refuge from her parents' turbulent marriage, in which she was often caught in the crossfire. She immersed herself in books and her own private fantasy world, to such an extent that Janet believed her to be a naturally undemonstrative child. Apart from their shared passion for horses, mother and daughter never enjoyed a close relationship.

Right: Jackie's sister, Caroline Lee Bouvier, was born on March 3, 1933. Jackie inherited her father's exotic looks, which served as an unwelcome reminder to Janet as the Bouviers' marriage disintegrated. Some harsh punishment was meted out to Jackie by her mother, physical as well as verbal.

The dapper Jack Bouvier was a feckless father, but instead of being shocked by his serial infidelity, Jackie was secretly impressed by her father's attractiveness to women. Although Jackie preferred his charm and zest for life over her mother's austerity, when the Bouviers divorced in 1940, Jackie and Lee continued to live with Janet.

Above: Jackie, aged ten, her mother (right), and a family friend attend a horse show in Tuxedo, New York.

Left: August 1949. Twenty-year-old Jackie (center) heads for France on a year-long exchange trip with some fellow students. Her father's Gallic roots fostered a passion for French culture and history. Such trips also offered an escape from her mother, with whom she clashed once again on the issue of education. Janet felt that academic qualifications might deter potential suitors. Jackie demurred, although on occasions she playfully feigned a lack of intelligence on dates to test the theory.

In January 1952 Jackie was appointed "Inquiring Camera Girl" at the *Washington Times-Herald*. She took her journalistic assignments seriously, although like her college contemporaries she was also aware of the need to make a good match. Her mother had joined the highest rank of society when she married Hugh Auchincloss, heir to the Standard Oil fortune, in 1942. Jackie had only a small allowance, however, and stood to inherit nothing.

Above: Jackie, pictured in 1953. At the beginning of the year her relationship with Jack was deepening. They attended President Eisenhower's Inaugural Ball together in January, the month in which Jack took his seat in the Senate. Twenty-three-year-old Jackie had already failed to follow the college-girl mantra—"Get the ring by spring"—and was keen to move things along with the Democratic Party's rising star. The pressure increased further when her sister Lee, almost four years her junior, married Michael Canfield in April of that year.

Above and right: The courtship was inevitably followed in the society pages, while *Life* magazine regularly featured the stunningly photogenic couple as romance blossomed. Sailing was Jack's passion, Jackie preferring country pursuits, including hunting.

In the spring of 1953 Jackie was still awaiting a proposal. At her mother's suggestion she traveled to London for Queen Elizabeth II's coronation. In letters home, and in her pieces for the *Times-Herald,* she described the glamorous social whirl of the smart London set. It was a crude, but successful, psychological ploy. Absence made Jack's heart grow fond enough to propose, although the vehicle—a telegram—was less than romantic. Jack was fascinated by Jackie rather than besotted. He still had a bachelor mentality, and it was Joe Kennedy who prompted his thirty-five-year-old son in the direction of marriage.

Left: Society beauties Jackie and Lee in formal attire. Jackie was self-conscious about aspects of her appearance, notably her broad shoulders and large hands and feet. These were invariably disguised through careful styling. Lee was petite and regarded as more classically beautiful—especially by Jackie herself—although she lacked Jackie's intelligence and wit. It was the older sister who possessed the indefinable quality that made her so attractive to men.

Right: Senator Kennedy and his fiancée leave LaGuardia Airport in June 1953 to spend the weekend at Cape Cod. The announcement of the engagement was a moment to savor for Jackie, as she could finally lay to rest her mother's jibes about her ability to attract a suitable husband. The Kennedys were not among the highest strata of WASP society, and had themselves been subjected to social exclusion, yet in terms of wealth and influence, they were among the country's elite.

The betrothed couple, pictured at Hyannis Port two days before their wedding. Several people had tried to warn Jackie that marriage to Jack was fraught with risk. Jackie was in love, smitten at the prospect of having won over "Washington's most eligible bachelor," as Jack was described in a *Saturday Evening Post* article shortly before the engagement was made public. She had already undertaken translation work to assist Jack in his senatorial duties. Intellectual stimulation was a vital part of the attraction, and Jackie believed this would be the template for married life. She was less enamored with the idea of a scavenger hunt for her engagement party. This was a typically boisterous Kennedy pursuit, and inevitably competitive—Pat Kennedy stealing a bus in an attempt to outdo the rest. Such pastimes were neither Jackie's style nor her forte.

Chapter Two

Jacqueline Bouvier Kennedy

Above: It wasn't long into the Kennedys' marriage before Jackie realized it would not be the fairytale union she had hoped for. She resolved to remain true to her vows, and the two shared a deep and abiding love that survived Jack's infidelity.

Opposite: Jack and Jackie were married at St. Mary's Church, Newport, Rhode Island, on September 12, 1953. The Auchinclosses wanted an understated affair, but Joe Kennedy insisted that the wedding of his eldest surviving son be a lavish occasion. It was certainly the society event of the year. For Jackie the day was tarnished by the fact that her father didn't give her away. Janet Auchincloss made it clear that her exhusband could attend the church ceremony, but would not be welcome at the reception. Jack Bouvier took solace in the bottle and missed the wedding, leaving Hugh Auchincloss to walk a devastated Jackie down the aisle.

bove and opposite top: The wedding reception took place at Hammersmith Farm, home of
the Auchinloss family. As Jack was now the undisputed star of his family, all the Kennedys put
his chosen bride under the microscope. Rose thought her eminently suitable initially, but the
two found they had little in common. Mealtime punctuality was a particular bone of contention,
Jackie's more relaxed attitude not finding favor with the punctilious Rose. Jackie got on famously
with her father-in-law, who regaled her with stories of his colorful past. Jackie warmed to the
vibrant, roguish Joe, in whom she saw shades of her own beloved father.

Right: Jackie settles down for an evening of study with her new husband. She began married life full of optimism, planning to play an active part in supporting Jack's senatorial duties. She even took a political science class to improve her understanding of his work. It was a short-lived hope. Jackie found day-to-day politics tedious and, with Jack much in demand, spent a lot of time alone. The first year of marriage also brought private tragedy as Jackie suffered a miscarriage.

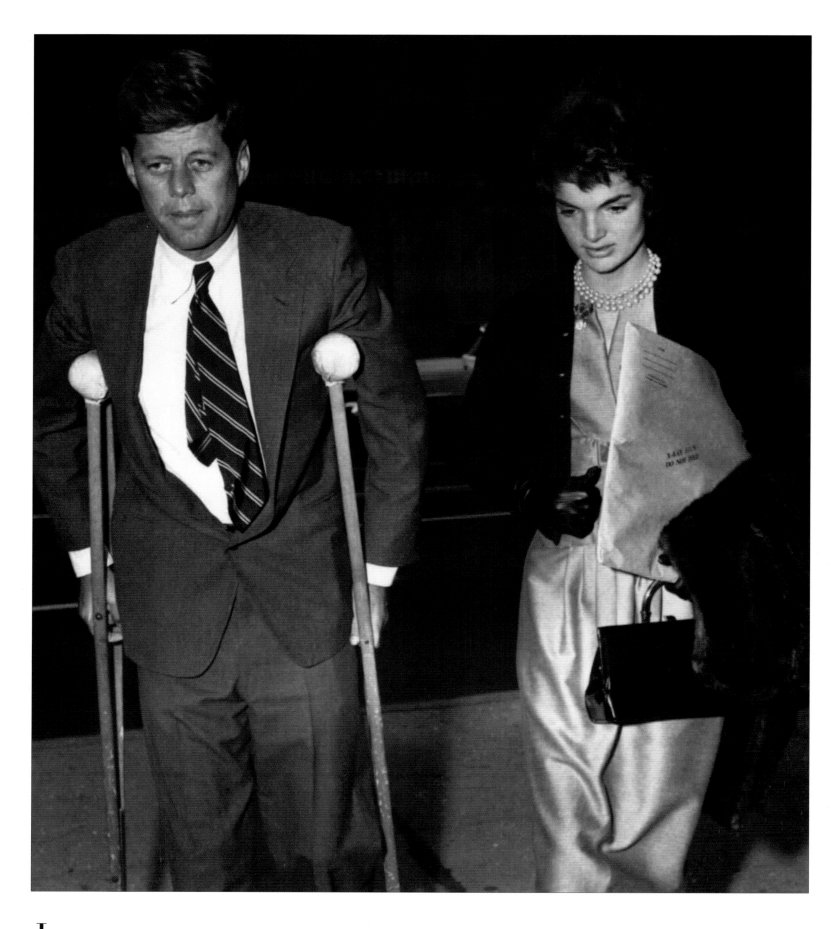

Jackie accompanies her husband following his discharge from the hospital on December 21, 1954. A year into the marriage Jackie found that her husband's celebrated athletic vigor was a myth. In October 1954 Jack was admitted to hospital to undergo a complex surgical procedure involving the fusion of vertebrae to alleviate his chronic back pain. The fact that he suffered from Addison's Disease made the procedure even riskier. An infection

set in and the last rites were administered. Jackie was a constant support throughout. She also showed she was learning the political ropes by playing down the seriousness of Jack's condition, rumors of which had reached the ears of his opponents on Capitol Hill. She also played a vital role in keeping Jack mentally stimulated, particularly in regard to his idea for a book about political figures who had shown courage in the face of adversity.

Left: Jackie at the 1954 April In Paris Ball with Sloan Simpson (left) and actress Celeste Holm. The charity event, held at New York's Waldorf Astoria Hotel, saw Jackie model a number of gowns from some of Paris's leading couturiers. Right up to the presidential election Jack thought that her refinement and expensive tastes might be a potential vote loser. He misjudged Jackie's appeal, which spanned both gender and social class.

Right: Jack and Jackie on the steps of the Capitol Building in May 1955 as the senator returns to work after his enforced eight-month medical leave of absence. The couple moved into a $125,000 house in McClean, Virginia, and Jackie put her creative talents to use on a grand refurbishment scheme. Her lavish spending would be a constant source of irritation to the famously parsimonious Jack.

ight: A girls' night out at the Stork Club in May 1956 to celebrate the forthcoming marriage of Jean Kennedy to Stephen Smith. Although the Kennedy family was firmly patriarchal, the females were expected to be as competitive and combative as their brothers. They didn't warm to Jackie, whom they dubbed "The Deb." She called them the "Toothy Girls." Left to right are: Jackie, Pat Kennedy Lawford, Ethel Skakel Kennedy, Jean Kennedy, and Eunice Kennedy Shriver.

Above: Dining out at the Stork Club, May 1955. Jack's long confinement put his tendency to stray temporarily off the agenda, and the marriage enjoyed a long period of stability and harmony. Once Jack had recovered, however, the cracks again began to show. In the summer and fall of 1955 the couple spent a considerable amount of time apart, and there were rumors of an imminent divorce. Jack and Jackie both considered this option, but over the following twelve months each pulled back from the brink and chose to commit to their marriage.

Opposite above: Jackie and Lee in model pose, circa 1955. When Jack's philandering resumed following his back surgery, a desolate Jackie heaped much of the blame on herself. The euphoria of the early days of married life was replaced by a feeling that her mother's view regarding her appeal might have been right after all. Jackie and her sister were especially close during this difficult period.

emocratic Convention, Chicago, August 13, 1956. Jackie and Eunice Kennedy Shriver watch the campaign film *The Pursuit of Happiness*, for which Jack provided the narration. He narrowly missed out on being selected as Adlai Stevenson's running mate for the November election, but his personal stock rose enormously, bringing a Kennedy victory in 1960 one step closer. After the convention, Jack wound down with a European vacation, leaving a heavily pregnant Jackie at home with her mother. She went into premature labor and gave birth to a stillborn baby girl. When Jack was finally contacted, he saw no reason to return home.

Caroline Bouvier Kennedy was born on November 27, 1957. After two tragedies, the arrival of a healthy child was a source of relief as well as unbounded joy to Jackie. Jack was infatuated with his baby daughter, and although fatherhood didn't curb his womanizing, it did strengthen the bond between him and Jackie. Caroline was named after Jackie's sister, whose full name was Caroline Lee, while the addition of her family surname was in honor of Jackie's father, who had died four months earlier.

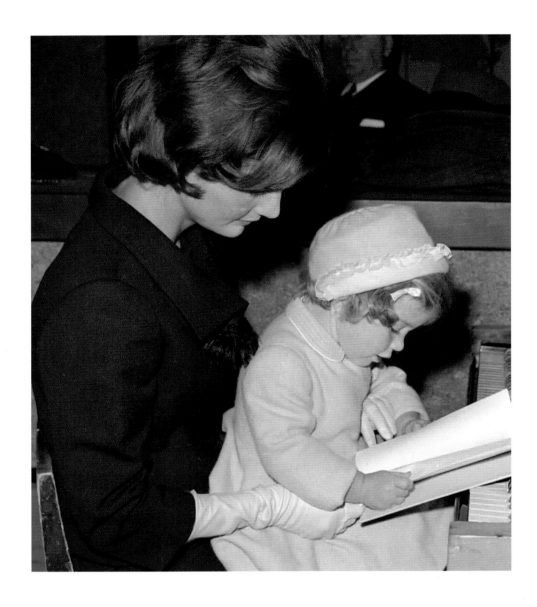

R ight: Jackie and Caroline wait for Jack to fulfill yet another speaking engagement. Jack's schedule from Caroline's birth through to the 1960 presidential election was punishing. "Plane" and "goodbye" were among the first words uttered by his daughter. Jackie was hugely supportive of her husband's bid to reach the White House, although she was much happier in the role of mother than campaigning wife.

B elow: After Caroline's birth the Kennedys took up residence in Georgetown. To help Jackie with the day-to-day domestic duties she employed an English nurse, Maud Shaw, who would remain with the family through the fateful events of November 1963. Jackie was reluctant to allow the media spotlight to fall on Caroline. Ever the political animal, Jack was far more sanguine about such matters.

Jackie looking radiant at the beginning of the 1960 presidential campaign. As Jack feared, his political opponents tried to make capital out of his wife's expensive tastes. Richard Nixon's wife, Pat, raised the issue of Jackie's liking for designer clothes. Jackie promptly defused the situation by appearing in a $30 off-the-rack maternity dress. It hardly mattered. Mrs. Nixon found—as Hubert Humphrey's wife had in the primaries—that the voters preferred a fairytale princess to someone they might meet on the street.

Jackie pictured in her home at 3307 N Street, Georgetown, a Federal-style house that the Kennedys acquired at the end of 1956.

Jackie pours tea for Democrat John Foley. All Kennedy females campaigned tirelessly, but none had Jackie's impact. Voters turned out in droves in the hope of merely catching a glimpse of the presidential candidate's wife. Jackie had played a crucial part in securing Jack's re-election to the Senate in 1958. She spoke of her campaigning in a TV program, *At Home with the Kennedys*, which aired shortly before the election. The combination of homespun values and glamor helped Jack win the biggest share of the vote ever seen in a Massachusetts senatorial election. Two years later the "Jackie factor" got Jack's presidential campaign off to a flying start until she was sidelined because of pregnancy.

Jackie, who had made few public appearances toward the end of the presidential election campaign because of her pregnancy, stands beside Jack as he delivers his acceptance speech at the Hyannis Armory on November 9, 1960. Jackie was ambivalent about being catapulted into the spotlight. She enjoyed the privileges high office brought, but remained an intensely private person. In particular she resented any intrusion upon her family life, especially where her children were involved.

Left: John, Jr., was born three weeks after Jack's election victory. On the day she came out of hospital Jackie toured the White House with outgoing first lady Mamie Eisenhower, despite being physically and emotionally drained.

Below: The Kennedy clan celebrates Jack's electoral victory at Hyannis Port, November 10, 1960.

Chapter Three

Queen of Camelot

Opposite: The first official portrait of the new first lady shows how much the camera loved Jackie. Requests for such photographs flooded into the White House. Jackie came to resent her every word and look being captured on film or tape. "I want to live my life, not record it," she once said.

Above: Jackie had already won over the Parisian crowds when she attended a state banquet at the Palace of Versailles in a stunning Givenchy evening gown. For political reasons she did not usually wear clothes by her favorite French designers; on this occasion she made an exception, with spectacular results.

Above: The look adopted by Jackie was reported at length in the style pages of the world's press. She appointed Oleg Cassini as her official designer, and on Inauguration Day his creations were the famous woolen coat and pillbox hat, and a white satin gown for the evening's gala celebrations. Jackie was not a great fan of millinery and grudgingly wore the hat, which she felt was the least unflattering of all the choices. But although she was largely unenthusiastic about the look, millions of women rushed to hat shops to copy it.

Opposite top: Even though Jackie wasn't in good health on Inauguration Day, she still managed to look radiant at a concert organized by Frank Sinatra, who had worked hard for a Kennedy victory. The singer adapted a favorite song with a rendition of "That Old Jack Magic," but for once he found himself upstaged; it was Jackie everyone wanted to see.

Right: Lady Bird Johnson was said to be incandescent when her husband accepted the vice-presidency. She was extremely fond of Jackie. Lady Bird deputized for Jackie on numerous occasions in the latter stages of the presidential campaign, when pregnancy forced her to take a back seat. Their friendship endured after Jack's death.

ight: The president and first lady play host to Prince Rainier and Princess Grace of Monaco on May 24, 1961. When Jack was recovering from his back operation in 1955, Grace Kelly, then a movie star, had donned a nurse's uniform and visited him in the hospital as a joke.

elow: Jackie looking radiant next to Nina Khrushchev (center). At a state banquet held at Schönbrunn Palace in Vienna, the Soviet leader found that the first lady's intellect matched her beauty. "Smitten Khrushchev Is Jackie's Happy Escort" one American newspaper headline read the following day.

Jackie with Lady Dorothy, the wife of British prime minister Harold Macmillan, on June 5, 1961. This was the final leg of a state visit which had taken the Kennedys to Paris and Vienna. In the Austrian capital Jack was given a lesson in international politics by Soviet leader Nikita Khrushchev, an experience that left him shell-shocked. Meanwhile, Jackie captivated Khrushchev and later, French president Charles de Gaulle. The Parisian crowds chanted, "Vive Jacqui!" to the first lady, who felt she was visiting her spiritual home.

Above: Queen Elizabeth II and the Duke of Edinburgh receive the president and first lady at Buckingham Palace on June 5, 1961. The Kennedys stayed with Jackie's sister Lee and her husband, Stanislaus Radziwill, during their London visit. Protocol dictated that divorcees could not be invited to a state function, but the queen waived this convention and allowed the Radziwills to attend.

Opposite: June 6, 1961. Jackie stayed in London at the end of the state visit, while the president returned to Washington. This European trip made Jackie a star on the international stage as well as at home. Attempts to recreate the "Jackie look" even extended behind the Iron Curtain.

ight: Police were needed to control the crowd that gathered outside Buckingham Palace to catch a glimpse of the first family. Jack himself quickly realized that it was Jackie most people came to see.

elow: A wave from nephew Anthony, son of Lee and Stanislaus Radziwill, during Jackie's London stay. Despite her sure-footed performance in a trip that took in five countries, Jackie remained ambivalent about the role of first lady.

Right: Jackie was again the center of attention when she took a short vacation in Greece in June 1961, taking up a personal invitation from Prime Minister Constantine Karamanlis. Jack admired and respected the aplomb she had shown on the world stage.

Left: President Kennedy practiced hard to perfect his famous "Ich bin ein Berliner" speech. Jackie, on the other hand, had a great facility for languages. Here she delivers a speech in perfect Spanish in Venezuela, in December 1961.

Left: In March 1962, Jackie, with her sister acting as a companion, embarked on her first official solo trip abroad, to India and Pakistan. The tensions between the two countries meant that even a seasoned diplomat would have been tested. Jackie carried it off superbly.

Below: Antique hunting was a particular passion for the first lady. Here, Jackie buys some eighteenth-century French china from one of her favorite shops in England's capital.

Jack marked Jackie's return to the United States at the end of March 1962 with a banquet to celebrate the success of her solo diplomatic trip. He also organized the transportation of Sardar, a horse that had been presented to the first lady by the prime minister of Pakistan.

Right: Jackie takes John, Jr., for a walk in April 1962, accompanied by the Empress of Iran. John was born prematurely and suffered from hyaline membrane disease. Patrick Bouvier Kennedy, born in August of the following year, would suffer from the same respiratory condition.

Left: When she became first lady, Jackie was appalled by the state of the White House décor. She took it upon herself to restore the presidential home to the grandeur of a bygone era. TV cameras were allowed in to see the fruits of her labors, with Jackie acting as hostess. She won the admiration of both her husband and the nation for a stunning transformation.

In the spring of 1962 the president and first lady hosted several state visits, including one by French Minister of Culture and novelist André Malraux. Jackie, a great admirer of his writing, wanted the United States to emulate France by introducing a ministry dedicated to the arts. Jack's cultural interests were more lowbrow. At White House receptions he sometimes had to be prompted as to whom certain artists were and in which field they excelled.

Left: In the summer of 1962 Jackie and Caroline traveled to Italy for a vacation, with Jackie's sister and brother-in-law. As always, the world press was out in force. Jackie loathed the goldfish-bowl aspect of her position: many column inches were even given over to debate whether it was seemly for a first lady to be photographed in a bathing suit.

Right: Jackie and Lee in Italy in August 1962. The jet-set group included Gianni Agnelli, heir to the Fiat fortune. A carefully cropped picture that appeared in the American press gave the impression that he and Jackie had dined alone one evening. Jack was concerned with the political fall-out of such images, and sent a terse telegram: "Less Agnelli, more Caroline." There was never a suggestion that Jackie responded in kind to Jack's infidelity.

Left: June 29, 1962. The president and first lady leave for a state visit to Mexico.

Below: Jackie's passion for horses was passed onto Caroline and John, Jr., from an early age. In the fall of Jack's second year in office the civil rights issue exploded in Mississippi, while the Cuban missile crisis brought the world to the brink of nuclear conflagration. The president did not discuss political issues with the first lady, but she was a vital source of support and comfort during an intensely stressful period.

Above: Caroline would follow her mother and become an accomplished horsewoman. As John, Jr., grew he enjoyed leisure pursuits that carried an element of risk. Flying would be a particular passion, but his fearful mother made him promise not to train for his pilot's license, a request he honored during her lifetime.

Opposite: When the first lady adopts a new hairstyle for the visit of Venezuelan president Romulo Betancourt, the photographs immediately adorn the style pages of the world's press. The American president was somewhat less enamored with the cost of being married to a fashion icon, which exceeded $100,000 per year.

J ackie's overriding concern was for her children to enjoy as normal an upbringing as possible. She set up a school that was attended by Caroline and children of members of the White House staff. Jack also encouraged the children to play in the corridors of power, including inside the Oval Office.

Above: Jackie celebrated her thirty-fourth birthday on July 28, 1963. She spent her days painting and reading, preparing for the birth of her third child in September. News that an agreement had finally been reached on nuclear weapons testing was a further cause for celebration in the Kennedy family. On August 7 the joyous period came to an abrupt end when Jackie was rushed to the hospital with abdominal pains. She underwent an emergency cesarean-section operation.

Right: August 14, 1963. United in grief, Jack and Jackie leave Otis hospital after newly-born Patrick Bouvier Kennedy loses his fight for life. Jackie declined the offer of a quiet rear-door exit, nor did she don her trademark dark glasses. Commentators noted the fact that the normally undemonstrative couple left the hospital hand-in-hand, and the tragedy did bring them closer together.

Left: Dallas was the fourth stop on the November 1963 two-day tour of Texas. The earlier visits had shown that Jackie was as popular as ever with the public and would be the ace in Jack's hand for the 1964 election.

Below: Jackie receives a bouquet of red roses as the presidential plane touches down at Dallas' Love Field Airport. Jackie had had some bad press over the recent European trip, particularly reports of revelry aboard Aristotle Onassis's yacht. On her return she was determined to play an active role in Jack's re-election campaign, beginning with the trip to the politically volatile Lone Star State.

The motorcade on its way to central Dallas, where the president was to make a speech at the Trade Mart. The clear blue skies meant that the protective bubble on the Lincoln convertible had been removed. The route the motorcade was to take had been printed in the local press the previous day. As the Lincoln turned into Dealey Plaza, shots rang out and Jack was struck by two bullets. Jackie cradled his head as they sped to Parkland Hospital, but the president could not have survived such terrible injuries, and was declared dead at 1:00 p.m.

Above: Jackie stands at Lyndon B. Johnson's side as he is sworn in as the thirty-sixth president of the United States. She refused to change out of her blood-spattered pink woolen suit, determined that the world should see the appalling, unvarnished aftermath of the assassination.

Opposite above: At Jackie's prompting John, Jr., performs a perfect salute for his father, something he had never quite managed before. Jackie's final gift to Jack—and the nation—was to organize the tableau of the funeral. The image of Jackie herself, regal in bereavement, endeared her even more to the American people and the wider world.

Left: Arlington Cemetery, November 25, 1963. Bobby Kennedy stands at Jackie's side for her husband's interment. The two would be a source of mutual support and comfort in the following months. "May the angels, dear Jack, lead you into paradise," said Cardinal Richard Cushing, who had also officiated at Jack and Jackie's wedding ten years earlier.

Chapter Four

Abdication

Above: Hyannis Port, March 1964. In the wake of Jack's death Jackie's overriding concerns were the welfare of her children and the glorification of the golden Camelot era.

Opposite: Jackie accompanied by the Duke of Edinburgh. She had been invited to attend many memorial services for her husband, but declined most. However, she was deeply touched by the ceremony at Runnymede in England. The site was steeped in history—a subject for which she and Jack shared a passion. She was also swayed by the fact that Harold Macmillan, Jack's mentor and her great friend, had agreed to give an address.

Left: Jackie picks up Caroline and her niece, Sydney Lawford, from the Convent of the Sacred Heart School, on Manhattan's East Side, in September 1964. Jackie had just relocated to New York City from Washington, D.C., where the memories were too painful, and the intrusiveness of the public had become intolerable.

Right: Jackie and John, Jr., visit the New York campaign headquarters of Bobby Kennedy, who had moved to New York in order to run for the Senate. Eventually Jackie would be enthused at the thought of her brother-in-law carrying on Jack's work as the country's chief executive.

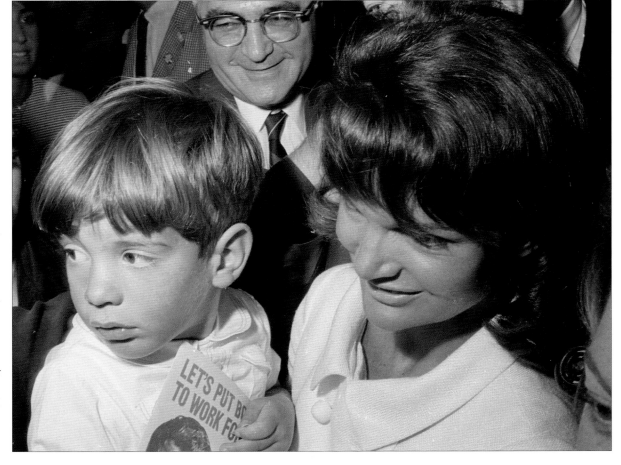

ight: Jackie gives John, Jr., a helping hand as he takes to the slopes for the first time. John-John's tender age lessened the impact of his father's death. In adulthood he would have no recollection of the funeral, or the famous salute that became an enduring symbol of a national tragedy.

elow: Aspen, December 1964. Although over a year had elapsed since Jack's death, media interest in Jackie's every move continued unabated. Reports even included details of her daily mealtime menu. Her grief had been played out in front of the camera, and so would her attempt to rebuild her life without Jack.

Above: Jackie with Princess Grace of Monaco at the annual gala ball held at Seville's Casa de Pilatos in April 1966. Shortly after the assassination the princess had visited the White House to offer her condolences. Jackie declined to see her. She still harbored a degree of jealousy over Jack's supposed feelings for the movie star a decade earlier.

Left: Jackie attends a performance of *On A Clear Day You Can See Forever*. Her escort was Alan Jay Lerner, writer-composer of Jack's favorite musical, *Camelot*. The line "Don't let it be forgot that for one brief shining moment there was Camelot" came to be associated as much with the Kennedy presidency as with musical theater.

ackie takes John, Jr., (left) and her nephew, Anthony Radziwill, for a stroll in a London park. Jackie turned down the chance of entering public life in her own right when she declined President Johnson's offer of an ambassadorial role. Relations between Johnson and the Kennedy clan were frosty, and it was only after Jackie's intercession that the president agreed to rename Idlewild Airport and Cape Canaveral after his predecessor.

eft: Jackie, Caroline, and John, Jr., with Queen Elizabeth II; David Orsmby Gore, a longstanding friend; and the Duke of Edinburgh (right) at the steps of the Runnymede monument. The site of the monument at Runnymede, where King John signed the Magna Carta in 1215, was ceded to the United States in perpetuity by Queen Elizabeth II. Jackie greatly approved of the memorial trust scholarship that was instituted, through which British students were able to further their education in the United States.

ight: Jackie and her brother-in-law, Stanislaus Radziwill. It was Lee Radziwill who first captivated Aristotle Onassis. The two had a love affair, but the shipping magnate came to regard J.F.K.'s widow as the more desirable woman, and the greater prize.

pposite: On the streets of London with sister Lee in May 1965. Jackie was slowly trying to cast off her widow's weeds. There was no shortage of suitors, and she came close to marrying Jack Warnecke, the architect who had worked on her husband's monument at Arlington Cemetery.

Above: Jackie examines plans for the proposed Kennedy Center for the Performing Arts with long-time friend Joan Braden.

Right: Jackie wears a traditional Andalusian outfit for a day's riding during her stay as a guest of the Duchess of Alba in Seville, April 1966.

Right: Jackie and John, Jr., in Honolulu in June 1966. Jack Warnecke, Jackie's new love interest, had been commissioned to design Hawaii's new government building and the couple spent several weeks together that summer. Jackie enjoyed security and privacy on the island and considered buying a house there. When the romance fizzled out, the dream of a home on the island paradise also faded.

Below: In the mid-1960s Jackie re-emerged as an international socialite. At the same time, she assiduously pored over the millions of words that were being written about Jack's life and work, correcting proofs where she felt the author had not done justice to his subject. She had regained her optimism for the future, yet was ever mindful of her role as custodian of J.F.K.'s legacy.

L eft: Jackie in jovial mood after meeting Emperor Haile Selassie in New York in February 1967. Ethiopia's leader had paid a state visit to the United States in the fall of 1963, and admired the courage Jackie had shown in undertaking her public duties despite her recent bereavement. They renewed their friendship weeks later at Jack's state funeral.

B elow: March 17, 1965. Jackie and Bobby Kennedy bid *bon voyage* to British ambassador David Ormsby Gore and his wife Sissie as they return to Britain aboard the *Queen Mary*. The Ormsby Gores had spent four years in Washington and became great friends of both Jack and Jackie.

Above: Jackie and her children received a rapturous Irish welcome when they arrived in Waterford for a vacation in June 1967. Jackie took Caroline and John, Jr., to Dungannon, from where their great-great-grandfather, Patrick Joseph Kennedy, had emigrated to America in 1858. Jack had made the same pilgrimage to County Wexford in the summer of 1963.

Right: Jackie gets the red carpet treatment during her goodwill visit to Cambodia in 1967. She was accompanied by David Ormsby Gore—now Lord Harlech. Following the recent death of Ormsby Gore's wife Sissie, he and Jackie's friendship deepened. They didn't marry, as many expected, but remained lifelong friends.

A bove: Jackie visits Bobby's New York campaign headquarters in May 1968. Her brother-in-law was riding high in the opinion polls and had just secured victory in the Indiana primary. "Won't it be wonderful when we get back in the White House?" she said, unable to contain her excitement at the thought of a second Camelot.

R ight: Jackie at prayer in St. Patrick's Cathedral, where Robert Kennedy's body lay in state following his assassination. When Bobby announced his intention to run for president in March 1968, Jackie was both elated and filled with a sense of foreboding. Three months later her worst fears were realized when Bobby was shot dead in the Ambassador Hotel, Los Angeles, having just won the crucial California primary.

J ackie and her children are joined by the Radziwills in a graveside vigil for Bobby. Jackie was already being courted by Aristotle Onassis, and Bobby's death made her more determined than ever to leave the perceived violence of America behind her.

Chapter Five

Regaining the Crown

Opposite: October 19, 1968. Jackie, Caroline, and John, Jr., take a stroll on the Greek island of Skorpios on the eve of her wedding to Aristotle Onassis. Jackie's marriage to Onassis, and self-imposed exile from America's shores, lasted for seven years. After the tycoon's death in 1975, she returned home, and effortlessly regained her crown.

Above: Jackie represented the ultimate conquest to sixty-two-year-old Onassis. He had an acquisitive attitude toward women and had courted a succession of beautiful women, including diva Maria Callas.

Above: Thirty-nine-year-old Jacqueline Bouvier Kennedy becomes Jacqueline Kennedy on October 20, 1968, in Skorpios, Greece. Only eight representatives of the world's press were given dispensation to attend. To Jackie this was a welcome indication of the fact that Onassis's wealth could outmaneuver unwanted media intrusion. It rained prior to the ceremony, a good luck sign according to Greek superstition. But unfortunately, the marriage turned sour long before Onassis's death in 1975.

Opposite: Jackie takes a tour of her new island dominion with John, Jr. Her new home on Skorpios offered her the peace and security she craved. Though not as handsome as Jack, Onassis had charisma, and Jackie embarked on married life for the second time full of optimism.

eft: Most of the Kennedy clan—and the American public—regarded Jackie's decision to marry Onassis as a betrayal of Jack's memory. "Anger, Shock, and Dismay"—the *New York Times*'s verdict—reflected the prevailing mood. The coarse, ruthless tycoon had one prominent advocate in Rose Kennedy, pictured here with her former daughter-in-law in the Bahamas in 1969. Rose gave the union her blessing.

ight: Jackie with her step-daughter Christina Onassis. Both Christina and her brother Alexander were bitterly opposed to the marriage. The antipathy toward Jackie became even more intense after a spate of family misfortunes, including Alexander's death. Superstitious locals laid the cause at Jackie's door. It was a new experience for Jackie to be the subject of vilification instead of adulation.

pposite: Jackie, pictured in the early days of her marriage to Onassis, when the relationship enjoyed harmony and contentment. For her fortieth birthday he gave Jackie jewelry worth over one million dollars.

Jackie poses during a visit to Lee's home in Oxfordshire, England, in 1968. With them is renowned ballet dancer Rudolf Nureyev, a close family friend.

Above: Jackie and Lee, pictured in 1969. Lee tried her hand at acting during this period, but her performances brought little acclaim, merely the accusation that she had been employed for her celebrity status—as sister of one of the world's most glamorous and admired women.

Left: Jackie and John, Jr., attend a memorial mass for Bobby on the first anniversary of his death. An early guest on Skorpios was Bobby's eldest daughter Kathleen. Bobby had promised her a trip to Europe after her graduation, and Jackie made sure that the pledge was honored. Had Bobby lived, and become the second Kennedy to occupy the White House, Jackie's life might have taken a radically different course.

Opposite: Jackie antique hunting in London in 1971. There were many parallels between her two husbands: both were charismatic, rich, powerful, older men that recognized and admired her qualities but unfortunately, were not monogamous. Jackie even launched into a grand refurbishment scheme of the Onassis family home on Skorpios, reminiscent of her days in Washington.

Left: Jackie on her way to a shipyard in Belfast, Northern Ireland, where Onassis was to inspect two new tankers that would soon become part of his empire. The tycoon believed that big business was a male domain, just as politics had been a male preserve for the Kennedys.

Jackie and fourteen-year-old Caroline on one of many foreign trips. Jackie's frequent travels eventually began to irk Onassis. His own numerous overseas visits combined business with pleasure, yet he balked at Jackie's long absences. Onassis did make an effort to have a good relationship with his step-children, Caroline and John, Jr., in contrast to his children, Christina and Alexander, who were openly hostile to Jackie.

Left: Jackie was the perfect hostess when Onassis entertained guests. Her sophistication and refinement were the perfect foil to his brashness and uncouth manner. She became the supreme business wife, just as she had been the ultimate political wife.

Below: On vacation in Egypt, 1974. As Jackie approached her forty-fifth birthday, Onassis—famously fickle and acquisitive with women—began to lose interest. He was now actively seeking a way out of the marriage at the least possible cost to himself. Prior to his death on March 15, 1975, Onassis had his lawyers working on a divorce settlement that would have cost him a sizeable share of his fortune.

Above: Twelve years after she won universal admiration for her conduct at Dallas and Arlington, Jackie mourns the death of Aristotle Onassis on March 18, 1975. Flanked by her two children and Teddy Kennedy, Jackie is again the epitome of dignity in the face of bereavement. The grief was not so palpable this time, not least because she was aware of Onassis's plans to divorce her. Even so, her second husband held a place in her heart, and she promised her step-daughter Christina that she would keep and honor the Onassis name.

Right: Many Americans cooled toward Jackie during her seven-year absence. She began to win them over again when she returned to the country in 1975. Almost immediately, she became a passionate advocate for preserving one of New York's great landmarks, as she took up the cause to save Grand Central Station from developers. Her tireless campaigning earned her much praise from the city's inhabitants.

eft: Jackie at a Thanksgiving Day hunt in New Jersey in 1976. After a protracted legal wrangle she won a settlement of some twenty-six million dollars from the Onassis estate. By the time the lawyers had reached an agreement Jackie had begun a new life back in New York. A number of revelations had begun to tarnish the image of Camelot, yet Jackie retained a special place in the country's affections.

elow: Jackie at a social function in 1977. Now in her late forties, she still attracted a succession of suitors, and embarked on several love affairs. She also took a job as a book editor at Viking publishing house, a first foray into paid employment since her days as a photojournalist over a quarter-century earlier.

Left: Jackie, pictured in her office at Viking with copies of the first major book project she saw through to publication. Its theme was Russian costume in the days of the czars. The publication of such a book would not in itself constitute a media event, but the newspapers were keen to run the story of its famous editor.

Below: On June 5, 1980, Jackie, John, Jr., and Teddy Kennedy look on proudly as Caroline graduates from Radcliffe College, Harvard, with a degree in fine arts. Afterr graduation she began work at the Metropolitan Museum of Art, where she met her future husband, cultural historian Edwin Schlossberg. The couple married July 8, 1986. Jackie became a grandmother three times over with the births of Rose, Tatiana, and Jack.

Above: A gathering of the Kennedy clan at Hyannis Port in December 7, 1980. Jackie gave unswerving support for Teddy Kennedy's bid to reach the White House that year. She played a major part in helping him secure victory in the New York primary, but such results were not replicated throughout the country and the campaign ended in failure.

Left: By 1984, when this picture was taken, Jackie had found personal and professional fulfillment. She left Viking to join another publishing house, Doubleday, in 1978. Her new employers appreciated the fact that she took her work seriously and did not try to exploit her celebrity status. She also found love with diamond merchant Maurice Tempelsman, whom she had known since her days in the White House.

Right: Jackie travels to Britain on January 31, 1985, for the funeral of one of her oldest and dearest friends, Lord Harlech, who had been killed in an automobile accident. She immediately set to work establishing the Harlech Scholarship in memory of the former British ambassador to the United States, with whom she enjoyed a close relationship after Jack's death.

Below: Jackie, John, Jr., and Caroline at the Kennedy Library, which opened its doors for the first time on October 21, 1979. Eighteen-year-old John, Jr., spoke in public for the first time at the dedication ceremony, reciting Stephen Spender's poem "I Think Continually of Those Who Were Truly Great." The library, an imposing glass edifice overlooking Dorchester Bay in Massachusetts, became another fitting tribute to the Kennedy presidency.

A bove: Jackie is joined by John, Jr., Teddy Kennedy, and Caroline for the dedication ceremony of J.F.K. Park in Cambridge, Massachusetts, a short distance from his alma mater Harvard University. Maurice Tempelsman had by now separated from his wife and eventually moved into Jackie's Fifth Avenue apartment, but they did not marry.

eft: As first lady Jackie won the hearts and minds of people everywhere, from world leaders to ordinary men and women. The courage she showed in the face of tragedy only served to deepen the affection in which she was held.

Opposite: The days of Camelot were long over, the jet-set lifestyle a thing of the past; yet the unrivaled elegance and style remained.

Conclusion

On May 18, 1994, when it was clear that the end was near, Jacqueline Bouvier Kennedy Onassis surrounded herself with the twin pillars that had sustained her throughout her life: family and books. Caroline and John, together with Maurice Tempelsman, held a constant vigil, reading selections of her favorite poetry as she slipped in and out of consciousness. She bore the last twenty-four hours of her life with the same stoicism, dignity, and majesty that had symbolized a nation's grief thirty-one years earlier.

By many standards, Jackie's achievements were modest. She had no great affection for the role of first lady, particularly for the way in which it impinged on the privacy of her and her children. Even so, she discharged her public duties with a grace and aplomb

the likes of which had never been seen. Her appeal crossed the boundaries of gender, wealth, and class; world leaders and blue-collar workers were equally captivated. On trips abroad crowds strained to catch the merest glimpse, though the United States remained her true dominion.

But there was more. Like her husband, Jackie transcended any attempt to define her role by the balance-sheet method. Just as John F. Kennedy represented much more than he accomplished, so Jackie stood for the beauty, elegance, and style that were the hallmarks of their thousand-day tenure at the White House. While Jack provided the political vision, Jackie was the soul of the Camelot idyll. Under her guiding hand the seat of power played host not just to statesmen, but to luminaries of the arts, including Stravinsky, Casals, Frost, and Steinbeck. In restoring

the White House to the glory of a bygone age she made the nation aware of the importance of rising above the merely functional and utilitarian. In short, Jackie ensured that the thirty-fifth presidency was a cultural beacon as well as a political watershed.

Following the events of November 22, 1963, it was as if the hopes the nation had invested in J.F.K. now rested on his grieving widow. The regal fortitude with which Jackie bore her loss gave America the strength and courage to preserve what was lost and to embrace the future. The pattern for this was laid down in her role as a mother. Jackie carefully guided Caroline and John through to adulthood, making them aware of their place in history, but ensuring they were not encumbered by it. It was a journey that included a self-imposed abdication, but she returned to the country where she had held court to find the affection of her people undiminished.

Millions across America listened as Jackie's funeral service was broadcast from St. Ignatius Loyola on Park Avenue in Manhattan, the church where she had been baptized and confirmed. The wheel had come full circle in more ways than one. The nation once again united in reverence, this time for the indomitable woman who had stood beside Lyndon Baines Johnson at his swearing-in ceremony, the woman who had refused to change out of her blood-spattered suit so that the world could see what they had done to her beloved husband. After the service she was buried next to John F. Kennedy at Arlington Cemetery. Thirty-one years after she lit the eternal flame for Jack, it now burned for both of them.